The Love Lottery

*a comic tale of lessons in life, love,
dating and the odd samosa party*

Raj Dhaliwal

Clink
Street

London | New York

Published by Clink Street Publishing 2018

Copyright © 2018

First edition.

ISBNs: 978-1-912262-70-0 paperback, 978-1-912262-71-7 ebook

Wannabe Girl Whisperer

'To figure out women is the equivalent of solving a Rubiks cube, blindfolded whilst suspended upside down!'

Quote formulated whilst drunk (a state when we are at our most informative and creative) on a night out in a Gentleman's club with close friend and colleague David Jones. RIP buddy.

Background

I am not a writer. Never have been. After having written this I don't think I could be, or would want to be, or more importantly asked to be. I am a humble accountant at a British-based automotive manufacturer of luxury vehicles.

There will be more caveats in this than in a legal document!

This is a light-hearted and hopefully humorous look at my dating exploits of past and sometimes present. It is in no way a guide on 'how to' or what you should or should not do, but merely a chance for me to share my experiences and hopefully some may mock, laugh or share some of those delightful experiences too.

I am not a pick-up artist or player in any way, shape or form. I wish I was, as my love life would have been a lot more colourful. More so than two shades of grey, let alone 50 shades of grey. I suppose I am one of many people out there who try and do anything and everything to find the other half, the missing piece of the puzzle, call it what you will. Yes, you've guessed it, I am desperate! I jest of course but I have come across many that are and I am desperate to not become one of them.

Dating in my teens to my mid-twenties was pretty easy and straightforward. Being married at 27 for seven years and then divorcing suddenly put me into a state of shock in terms of how the dating game had changed and moved on in such a short space of time. The same has been noted by the many I have spoken to about this. Was it evolution or a revolution? Depends on whom you ask.

Fortunately, I have tried to keep up with the evolution of dating over the last seven years and its various formats, and successfully avoided platforms such as Tinder etc., but am thankful I was only married for seven and not fourteen years. I would have been screwed otherwise and would have had to take a vow of celibacy and not out of choice!

Everyone I know is either married or in a long-term serious relationship and thus obtaining any form of advice is useless as they will be out of touch if they broke up also.

I, like many, have been bored of the same old lines such as:

"I promise you, there is someone out there for you" – where? Outer Mongolia?

"Be yourself, they will like/love you for who you are" – really!? Nope, I am gonna lie my backside off to add an air of mystique and cover the bullshit. Come clean eventually

if it looks like it may be going somewhere. I don't recommend this plan though.

"Be patient, you can't rush these things" – any longer and the equipment will gather cobwebs and stop working! They say patience is a virtue, therefore I must be the most virtuous man I know.

The good news is that it is easier meeting people nowadays. However, it seems to be a minefield. Tread carefully, very carefully. What could have been an innocent comment or the norm back in the early 00s is now taken out of context or vice versa.

In order to write about and share my experiences, I had to take out some much needed (me) time. The dating and meeting purposefully for a potential partner had to go on the backburner. This was gladly done out of choice.

I suppose, only writing about it will allow me time to contemplate and reflect and plan going forwards, re-energise and motivate almost. That and also to highlight my own experiences and throw it out there and be judged. Well… it seemed like a good idea at the time.

The Indian Connection

What is the reason behind the name of the book? I was torn between two titles and had only decided upon the completion of it.

Well, to think it nearly could have been called *Indian Accountant, That Makes Me a Catch Right?* —that would have made the title come across as too long to remember and also me a tad narcissistic!

As for *Wannabe Girl Whisperer*, yes I am wishing and dreaming but I was inspired by a line from a show and it has stuck in my head ever since.

Traditionally the Indian (Sikh) culture have always believed in, and are keen advocates of, education, and the professions that portray being unique or even elite to an extent. Bean counter is indeed the personification of sexy, but elite? Hmmm maybe. I jest of course. Ben Affleck in *The Accountant* has raised the sex appeal of Finance Demi-Gods no end! Or so I like to think.

Lawyer, doctor or accountant (the top three) were the traditional 'respectful' professions a typical Indian (Sikh) parent would have wanted to have their child follow. As times moved on, engineers, architects amongst many others etc., were being acknowledged as being up there with the top three. As times moved on, yet again the spectrum of top professions in the eye of the Indian parent became broader. This was emphasised by the size of the house So and So lives in, and the how new their Mercedes Benz is compared to everyone else's, or even how many BMWs they had parked in the drive.

Anyhow, my path was that of wanting to be an architect initially but falling into accountancy after having studied for an Accounting and Finance degree. Needless to say, mum n dad were chuffed!

Once having gained a degree and having started work, naturally the next step in the life plan was to find a 'suitable' partner and settle down and produce lots of mini-accountants! God help us!

Educated, working and single? Congratulations! You are now deemed 'suitable'!

That means you are now eligible for entry in to the world of function introductions and Samosa Parties! Entrance is free and you will be scarred for a short while afterwards but hey, everyone has experienced it! Coming to a weekend that you wanted to use to do something else much more interesting!

Function Introductions

For the benefit of those who are not of an Indian/ Sikh background, I shall try and explain the function introduction as generically as possible.

When spring and summer seasons arrive and the sun is out for more than five minutes, Indians cannot resist clogging up the family calendar with functions every weekend. Any thoughts of a social life or planning a holiday have to be done with the greatest of planning. Almost down to an art any project manager/planner would be proud of.

There are the usual functions such as engagements, weddings, babies birthdays, 18th and 21st birthdays and for the tight-fisted bunch (they prefer to be called frugal), there are the religious functions where the family don't have a party but a small gathering where we all just sit in the Gurdwara (Sikh Temple) and pray for forgiveness for our sins before committing a multitude of new ones upon departure. If we're lucky, we may even get a slice of cake at the end of it all.

Basically, imagine having gone to a family function and whilst trying to consume butter chicken (at a party) or chilli paneer (at a Gurdwara as meat is forbidden on the premises), you have a group of ladies or 'Aunties' (Matrimonial Intermediaries) watching you.

Trying not get freaked out but also trying not to make a mess, thoughts start running into your mind. *"Did I not say hello?"* or *"Do they know mum and dad?"* or even *"WTF?! I am famished and trying to worship the needs of my stomach right now! Be gone and leave me be!"*

Naturally, I just smile shyly and try to look angelic (bibba is the saying) whilst doing so.

Next thing you know, either one or both of your parents will approach you with an 'Auntie' (Intermediary) and ask you to look at a particular girl in the corner eating her food or standing there talking to family. Two things could be going through her mind when she notices a small group of strangers staring (squinting in my case as I am too vain to wear glasses when not in front of a laptop or tv) at her intently.

Optimistically, whilst trying to do my best pose and pout and showing my best side, I am hoping it's *"Oh! Why hello there handsome! pray tell, where have you been hiding?"*

Realistically, and on most occasions a facial expression can convey a thousand words and it can be more like *"WTF?! Oh man not again! Where are my parents?! These lot are freaking me out right now and I just want to go!"*

I know this as I met my ex-wife at one of these Function Introductions and that was what she was thinking every time this would happen to her.

On the odd occasion when the lady has been forewarned by her parents that a 'suitable' guy is here at the function with his parents and they would like to meet her, it's normally an awkward moment. Out of politeness she will agree to a quick chat and the fun starts.

Think of a covert operation but with Indian parents. Bless them. They try and come up with hand gestures and signals that an elite SAS/Navy Seal unit would be proud of in any undercover sting operation.

Rather than just say *"Come over here"* or *"Let's go over to that room or corridor where it's quiet and you two can talk"*, it becomes a *Give Us a Clue* session, minus Lionel Blair! *Give Us a Clue* is a British televised game show version of charades which was broadcast on ITV from 1979 to 1992. Lionel Blair was a tap-dancing team leader on the show from what I remember.

Anyhow, you end up standing there doing jerky half moves and not sure which way to go or whether to stay where you are. Thus ending up looking like one of the human robots you would see busking or performing on the Champs Elysee!

Why all the secrecy? Sikh Parents love to know all about everyone else and their business but don't want all and sundry knowing theirs generally. Agreed it's a sweeping generalisation but there are elements of it that are prevalent now and again.

The secrecy is to avoid any relatives or friends at the function asking questions later on about the fact their son or daughter was seen talking to another guy/girl when they are not related. *"Why are they talking?"*, *"How do they know each other?"*, *"They don't know each other?! Then why are they talking? Oh! Are you trying to get them married?"*. Then before you know it, relatives will have assumed the person you are talking to is now somehow a fiancé! Blooming Indians!

Then after the lady and I manage to talk, I have become Jason Bourne and start using peripheral vision to observe both my family and hers looking across trying to decipher if they think they are about to become in-laws. I can see the function hall and DJ mentally being booked. Occasionally one of the parents will try and walk past us both innocently as if to be on their way somewhere. Times like this you can tell they wished they had all the spy gear like James Bond/MI5/MI6 etc., or be a fly on the wall.

Then when it's all over, OMG! Greek tragedy or Indian Soap drama tragedy! (Even worse) the blood drains from their faces! The idea of what could have been, but will now never be, dawns upon them! Priceless! For everything else there is Mastercard!

Roll on next weekend for the yet another family function! Same time, same DJ (family discount applies), sometimes same people but different location!

Samosa Parties

For me, back in the late 90s and early 00s, there would be introductory events at an intermediary's home. I have always known them as Samosa Parties.

Again as before, for the benefit of those who are not of an Indian/Sikh background, I shall try and explain the Samosa Party.

These are not for the faint-hearted or indeed any shrinking violets. They can be daunting unless you become acclimatised to many and have subsequently built up a good immune system. The experience is the same, just a different house, different girl and if you are in luck a different recipe used for the samosas!

Picture the scenario. My parents and I have just pulled up in front of the girl's family home or the house of the Auntie who is trying to facilitate the pairing. If I am driving and I am feeling a tad brave or cavalier, I shall use the drive and make myself at home already!

The curtains/blinds in every window at the front of the house start to twitch. As we get out of the car, I hear voices. No not the ones in my head, they only come out on a Friday night after a couple of shandies! Numerous voices are heard, how many are living in this house? It's a bit *Walton's*!

Doorbell button is pushed. The door is cautiously opened. Why? Were they not expecting us? Anyhow, I decide to be a man and hide behind my parents and let them go in first.

As I walk in across the threshold, I scan around. Jeeeeessssssus! There are blooming Indians everywhere! They are hanging off the banisters on the landing, they are on the stairs, the entrance hall/reception is a tight squash anyhow as we get directed towards one of the rooms.

Blimey! There are even more of them in here!

Mum and Dad are directed towards the sofa. It feels like a group/family interview as we are surrounded by the girl's family and the Aunties' family too. In Punjabi I hear the obvious questions like *"Is he the boy?"*

There have been times when I have felt like responding in Punjabi with *"Nope, I am the Dad, my wife likes a toy boy and Mother Nature has not been too kind to my son!"*

I then would smile to myself and the audience (family members but feels like every move is being watched) would stare intently and wonder if I am actually on something. Try explaining to them you are high on life.

Then the awkward silence ensues. I have no idea why. Then one of the Uncles decides to break the silence and ask in Punjabi which route or motorway we used to get to the house and if we found it okay. Suddenly every male in the room decides that he is the Head Geographer and Oracle of Ordnance Surveys and the company that produced the A to Z maps is almost entirely dependent upon him for route guidance and traffic avoidance.

Then there is silence once again. The mothers and Aunties then perk up. After having ascertained I am the son, the key questions are then asked in Punjabi. *"What does your son do?"* followed by *"How old is your son?"* As far as I am aware, I can converse in clear and concise Punjabi but somehow feel like a small child who has been told to sit there, *"Be good and don't make a noise as mummy n daddy are talking to the grownups!"* I could have answered the questions myself but hey ho. Accountants should be seen and not heard.

After more silence, the samosas are ready! At this point the family normally get the girl in question to bring out the samosas and sometimes she may be assisted by someone else. There are times when the girl is assisted by her sisters, cousins, and sisters-in-law and whoever else is female! The issue is whom am I supposed to be checking out? There have been many a time when I have thought the sister-in-law or the cousin is the actual girl only to find the one I didn't feel an attraction towards is the one in question.

I have a code set with my parents for occasions like Samosa Parties. If I don't feel an attraction or connection with the girl, I will subtly nudge my dad. He then knows the score. I think by now he may have lost all feeling in his ribs from all the nudging I have done in days of past.

Then the ultimate question is asked in Punjabi. *"Would your son like to talk to our daughter?"* Always at the most inopportune time when I am a tad peckish and halfway through devouring a samosa!

Admittedly, there have been times when I have felt like saying *"Nope, thanks for asking and thanks for the samosas too! That accompanying chutney really brought out the tangy taste of the potatoes and softened the pastry that could have sliced my gums with the edges!"*

Instead, I would look over towards my dad, no point looking at mum as she would just smile and not do anything. If I had nudged him earlier, then he knew I would be back in five or ten minutes max. If I had not, then I would be back in half an hour and put my coffee on hold, Papa Bear!

I would occasionally glance over at my younger brother who used to accompany me in the earlier days for moral support which then subsequently turned into more of a mick taking session until he got bored and stopped coming along. He would just sit there and grin. I knew that grin would be a *"Rather you than me"* as opposed to *"Good luck bro, I am routing for ya! Bring back a bhabi!"* (bhabi means sister-in-law).

If I was in luck, I would get directed towards another room. If not, I would end up talking in a dining room or conservatory for all to view through the glass doors and look at my body language and level of flirtatiousness. I had no shame back then. Still don't!

After having finished our conversation, we would both walk in to where the family are sat. Not surprisingly the conversation amongst the rest of the family members on both sides is in full flow. The dads are like long-lost brothers and the mums and Aunties have bonded and really encapsulated the meaning of sisterhood.

Then the final silence of the day is upon us. It's detail swapping time. Phone numbers etc. are exchanged and promises made to phone on a certain day or date with regards to if the girl and I want to take it further and meet up again.

Looking back in fondness, it was so much easier back then to say no. The awkwardness was between the mums – the dads knew how to stay well out of this.

Everyone was happy when it was a no for both parties.

When it was a no from her and a yes from me, I was glad it was mum breaking the news to me followed by *"She looked like a bit of a bitch so it's her loss"*. Unbelievably mum would say that as she was naturally protective of her offspring.

If it was a yes from the girl and a no from me not surprisingly mum would say *"Not surprised, you're an accountant, so that makes you a catch!"* Hence the reason I nearly used this expression as the title for this book.

Mum is a Yorkshire lass, so she says what she likes and she likes what she bloody well says! As a Harry Enfield character once echoed.

Leap Into the Unknown

Not long after being divorced, I spent a couple of years being convinced and finding reasons why Indian ladies possessed the 'evil gene' based on the ones I had met, and thus undertook a United Nations Love Ambassadorial role and dated anyone regardless of ethnic origin or colour.

I was an active participant of this before I married an Indian lady and found it quite refreshing being immersed in different backgrounds once again. Just to clarify, I would have married anyone I wanted regardless of background and it just so happened that I met my ex-wife who happened to be Indian.

I for one never thought I would ever have to resort to internet dating. In fact my friends and I used to ridicule the whole concept and would stereotype the types of people who used to rely on it. How times have a changed and how karma is getting back at me for mocking so.

Whilst being married, for me internet daters were:

For a male, a freaky nerdy recluse or pervert or both who had only interacted with his mum in terms of female and aspired to being with the sort woman he had seen on porn sites. He would be unkempt, smelly and socially awkward especially with women and hide behind a sticky screen.

For a female, a Scraggy Maggy or scary cat lady. The one who has 20 cats with the same name and will not love or give any man the time of day unless he accepts her and her 20 cats with room for 10 more.

Immature and naive go with the general stereotype assumptions I know. That was back then.

It did not dawn on me at any time that these internet daters were just far too busy leading busy interesting lives and just did not have the time or energy to meet people due to being busy doing cool stuff.

They did not want the hassle of meeting the 'wronguns' and risking meeting people they did not know.

The dating sites, in the words of a lady I once met, *"Sifted out the crap and left you with a half decent chance."*

Traditionally, Indians who decide to become Matrimonial Intermediaries will look at things like education, profession, family background both in the UK and in the motherland, height, weight, etc., amongst general aesthetics for any potential pairing. They have done for hundreds of years probably. The Western society has caught on and taken it a step further with dating sites.

Since being divorced and having that label attached as a divorced guy who has hit the magic or tragic big 40, the function introductions and Samosa Parties have dwindled more and more. Thankfully the Samosa Parties more so, as they were never fun.

The fact that I am divorced suddenly provoked the thought and idea into the head of many a Matrimonial Intermediary commonly known as an 'Auntie' that I was somehow now desperate and would inevitably go for anything female with a pulse. The ensuing results were a multitude of mismatches.

As a result of these 'mismatches', I felt I had no alternative, due to lack of time and lounge lizard skills, to go online and explore the wonders that may be out there.

There was a point in time I was on more internet dating sites than I could remember. The only sites I wasn't on were Autotrader and eBay – no reserve, no bids!

I found it strange how we are so reliant upon formulas and algorithms on a dating site to determine whom we may consider to be our match.

Computer says no! The only real algorithm is our own human brain.

Let's Go Shopping!

The internet dating world, in my interpretation, is almost like shopping. In this case, imagine shopping for a used car.

The make and model may have already been defined (Indian Female or Caucasian Male for example).

The first most frustrating thing is there being a lack of photos or even one pic.

Are they that hot that they are inundated relentlessly with unwanted attention? Is anyone? It seems more and more apparent that we tend to live in a somewhat more fickle world and as much people may say looks are not everything, they are.

We need a photo to 'see what we are buying' and ascertain if the product is worth investing time and interest. Not a nice way to put it across I know but, it's the only plain and simple way to see it.

All that is left now is to go through the adverts (profiles with pics) and see what you can get for your price. The price being me and what I can attract as a package.

You will be mindful of things such as:

The specification. This can be whether that person be tall, short, slim, curvy, has a good job, etc. We all have our own desired specification and some options are essential such as a full head of hair whilst others not so much, such as a six-pack. Then again either or both could be expected standard features or not, depending on whom is being asked.

The age and condition. Do they look good for their age? Are they well maintained? Or do they look like they have had a hard life? More importantly do they look like the photo?

Look at service history. Does that person have more baggage than Heathrow Terminal 5? Have they had an abusive former partner, or a painful divorce, how many former partners? Not that it should matter but if they were married more times than Elizabeth Taylor then one cannot help but wonder.

Are there free accessories? Are there any children in the picture? Grown up or not. May or may not make a difference as many don't mind a readymade family but these details can sometimes be overlooked and not disclosed.

We will always come across the not so truthful adverts now and again. Slight omissions on the service history, spec and condition etc. and the *'sold as seen'* method is not always an appealing one unless one is in urgent need and cannot wait any longer.

To use a car analogy, yes... yet again despite knowing ladies don't really fancy being compared to a car, a woman is similar to certain types of car.

What type of car do I go for when shopping? It's all about the experience and what I want in the long run. The car being the lady of course and the driver being me.

Flashy so I look good but unreliable, temperamental and high maintenance?

Not so flashy but understated. Only I know of how good the attributes are and the appreciation is reciprocated in terms of reliability, fun to be with?

Quirky and different but appreciated and admired as a result of being individual and not mass produced? Potential classic dare I say?

There are cars that handle well. Very well in fact. This is regardless of conditions, time of day, month or year. The car can be pushed and pushed and always reward the driver (you) regardless of the level of natural skill or ability the driver may have. They leave you overwhelmed with the whole experience. The greed of reliving what has been and always wanting more with a heightened sense of anticipation and relishing the next encounter, no matter where or when. These cars do not have to be flashy or even desired by others. They are yours to cherish and love unconditionally despite bad times as they are outnumbered by the good with a ratio of 100:1.

Then there are cars that don't handle well at all. They may look the business or come across as easy to live with but disappoint. They cannot handle anything remotely challenging and no matter how skilled and experienced the driver, will just not respond. On the other hand there are those that are unpredictable and just snap out of control no matter what level of skill and experience the driver has. Some drivers like a challenge, other would prefer to walk away, look back at was has happened, what may have happened and be grateful the outcome was not worse.

The Profile

This is the downside and most daunting task one could undertake. After procrastinating, I would sit there for an age whilst logged in to a dating website or two contemplating.

I had to somehow combine persuasive language with the kind of images that made my profile float her boat rather than sink it, which, I as well as many have learned from experience, isn't as easy as it sounds.

"Pray tell, how on earth do I go about doing this? I've gotta look cool, I've gotta look fun, I've gotta look amazing, I've gotta look like I am THE ONE ladies have been waiting for all their lives! I can't look desperate! I am an accountant! Therefore, I am a Finance Demi-God! You can do this!"

I would muster all of my strength and self-control and focus my concentration to stop being distracted by thoughts of more interesting stuff to surf on the net. Porn! eBay! Autotrader! How to apply the minimum amount of coats of paint to obtain the maximum effect on a picket fence! Mating habits of otters! Anything so help me God!

I would like to say I had asked my friends for help on writing my profile. I didn't. Yes they may know me better than I know myself but the embarrassment was overwhelming. Besides, they would only make fun of me and be as useful as a chocolate teapot and would put me off the whole idea.

I knew one thing about writing my profile. I had to keep it short and sweet. No choice as certain websites would not let you write more than 300 words! How am I supposed to sell myself with only 300 words?!

"Accountant, Tall, GSOH, loves women and cars! I'm catch of the day so cast that net baby and reel me in!"

Yeah right! That might have worked in some parallel universe or the 80s, I'm guessing, but in no way was going to cut the mustard now.

Granted I wouldn't introduce myself to someone in a bar with my entire life history, but women would want to mentally vet someone when they meet them. Make sure he is not a weirdo, psycho or a man with a beard!

Honesty is the best policy! Lying doesn't get you anywhere in the dating world! I once read. Well... I suppose I am screwed then aren't I? As tempting as it was to inflate or sugarcoat certain attributes I managed to resist the urge. An example being, my love for cars entails me participating in track days and rally days, I resisted the desire to put down part-time racing driver!

I suppose both sexes want to find someone who can make them laugh. Well, most profiles request that attribute, *"GSOH is a must"*. Well ladies, I have a dry but FSOH – Fantastic Sense of Humour! I shall therefore show you people I have a sense of humour. If I can make someone laugh, it will be a great icebreaker. If they don't laugh at my jokes like I do, then they have none! Can't really put that in the profile but I shall make it representative of me somehow.

This brings me on to the 'shopping list'. I was tempted to say must have a fantastic bum when wearing jeans but could see the response rate being as low as a nuclear submarine in the Atlantic.

I didn't want to come off as a male diva or unrealistic. So, apart from the obvious items one would find on a list such as caring, intelligent, ambitious, kind etc. I had to add a few more adjectives. I struggled.

I tried to avoid clichés as much as possible. Even if I were to be a huge fan of something I thought it best to leave them out as it would provide me with more material in a conversation on the phone or as I like to call it the 'Telephone Interview' before meeting up.

I had noticed a lot of profiles had things like 'Walking on the beach despite living in rural Worcestershire', 'Surfing for porn', 'Drinking wine whilst staring at a roaring fire'. I mean who doesn't like doing these things?

This brings me neatly onto listing sociable hobbies. Once again I had to divulge a bit about me but not make it look like ladies had no choice but to imagine how they'll fit into my life. Describing one's self as a 'book-worm' or 'internet porn addict' (activities are not mine but described for extra effect) may make them feel they would hardly see me. Somehow, I had to play up my love of anything remotely sporty, or outdoor even if I would only partake on a full moon!

I had to learn to stay positive and avoid any form of negativity. My tone had to be positive. I once read that my profile is essentially my dating CV. I wouldn't want a future employer to read anything negative, so why would I want a potential partner to read anything that isn't positive? Very true.

So… the urge to do an eBay style of review and say *"Recently re-joined this website again! On here due to last lady being a timewasting cow!"* is not ideal. Truthful but on this one, honesty is not the best policy.

The final but crucial part of the profile is the picture/s. The decision on the type of pictures to take and then upload will either make or break the profile. Pressure's on!

I was advised to choose action shots. Great if I could demonstrate playing a guitar or downhill skiing but I could not do either. Air guitar or playing the triangle, even if my face isn't showing, isn't going to guarantee I receive more messages. Once again, I was screwed.

In addition, I had to choose recent photos. I have read many articles on internet dating before taking the plunge myself and one of the most frequent complaints about online dating profiles is how someone may have looked like once but they certainly don't look like it now. Naturally, looking better in the flesh is much better than the reverse. I was also informed that many ladies would rather see a big happy grin in a profile photo than a sexy pout. Basically, be an action man whilst laughing my head off at any dangers that may be in the way and looking good! No problem!

One thing I have noticed about my competition, other Indian guys, is the type of profile pics they have. I know this from the one's my female friends have forwarded on to me with the caption "Don't you dare use a profile picture like this guy!"

I am a gym bunny but my profile pic does not show it intentionally. I used a couple of natural shots my younger brother had taken on the sly. He subsequently emailed me the pics to use and I have received compliments on them as I do display a *'more cheese please Gromit'* style of cheesy grin.

However, these dudes have taken the art of posing up a notch. I have seen pics that have guys wearing sunglasses indoors, which I have been informed is a no no. Luckily I did not have any of those pics.

I have also seen guys in vests hanging out of convertibles with their arms tensed. The ones who are 'flexing' are so tensed they look as though they are about to 'shit one out' because the look on their faces are that extreme!

There are numerous dropdown boxes and filters and fields to fill in on a majority of the dating sites whether they be Indian or non-Indian ones. I have been informed on many an occasion that failure to fill in all fields or just have a cavalier approach to this does not bode well and can portray a 'cannot be bothered' attitude. If someone cannot be bothered to fill out their profile in full, can they be bothered at all?

The type of female I would go for has to be populated correctly. There is no dropdown box, filter or field that has the prerequisite *'nice down to earth personality with a fantastic bum'* or *'anything, I will go out with anything!'* What I did not want to have happen is the spectrum be too broad and all and sundry start connecting with me. Don't get me wrong, that would be absolutely fantastic, but that meant spending ages going through profiles and the whole task being arduous and a laborious one at best.

In the words of my best friend David Jones, *"I dunno much about art but I know what I like!"* This basically meant, I do not have a type but I know whom I would be attracted to as and when.

David had a theory. This was an important factor when it came to populating age range. Did I play it safe and possibly echo desperation by selecting 18-45+? I did not want to lose out to any potential love of my life due to a narrow margin.

Or did I adopt Dave's theory? The theory is a guy, providing he looks good for his age, can get away with dating or just being with a lady half his age plus seven. The proviso was the lady in question looked her age and did not like a teenager. So basically a 40-year-old guy with a 27-year-old lady. If the guy looked early thirties and the lady looked maybe a year or so younger than her real age, if that, then a perfect match. In theory anyhow. Dave was a tad quirky like me. We had no theory that could be attributed to females though.

Finally, checking grammar. Unless English is my fourth language behind Mongolian, Flemish and Punjabi, there is no excuse. Poor grammar and spelling is a turn off, and although the best of us can make mistakes, the profile can be entered into Microsoft Word alongside utilising the standard computer spellcheck for additional peace of mind.

Profile for a Friend

A close friend of mine made the mistake of asking me for some help on her online profile. I naturally rose to the challenge and relished the whole undertaking.

I had taken a look at some of her pictures she had taken whilst on holiday and noticed there was a nautical theme going on. She is not a yachtswoman or sailor but it was sheer coincidence she had those pictures and I had tried nautical puns on a speed dating event not so long ago.

I thought *"Sod it, let's go with it anyhow and see what happens!"*

It went a bit like this:

Ahoy there shipmates! Yo ho ho & a bottle of rum!

Shiver me timbers! I am all about life adventures and the exploration of all things new!

Finding love on the other hand, is a bit like fishing before a tidal wave! No smooth sailing at all.

There is a calm before the storm and the next thing you know, someone comes along and capsizes my dinghy without me having caught anything!!

Like most at this busy port of (name of dating site inserted), I am getting weary of rough seas and choppy waters on my travels on the ocean of love in my quest for that elusive one! It's all making me rather seasick!

I just want to set sail in my love boat and drop anchor with my bounty/treasure/catch of the day – call it what you will and share the adventures and new experiences together.

Now for the important bits. Please do not contact me if you are one of the following as these will be regarded as Pirates!

1) Not over the ex-Pirate in crime!

2) Window shopping and not serious about establishing a meaningful relationship – I need a fellow swashbuckler with matching boots!

3) Someone who thinks they can loot my bounty

4) Someone who ends up sinking my boat rather than float it – you must have an interesting & quirky personality

We all dislike Pirates and these irritating scoundrels will be made to walk the plank and given the old heave ho!!

If you fancy a trip of a lifetime and well-travelled life of adventure and fun then drop me a line, if not, then enjoy suburbia!

Aaarrrr!!!

Surprisingly, she did not get many responses from Indian men with this! I personally think the humour wasted on them and was a bit too Sahara desert for them.

What a World

Once it was: "Boy meets Girl," and, depending on circumstance, "Boy gets (or does not get) Girl." Now, it's Boy posts profile. Girl posts profile. Profile does or does not pique interest. Maybe Boy and Girl meet—or maybe they don't, and if they do, do Boy and Girl live up to their profiles and live happily ever after?

Cannot remember where this quote came from but I saved it on my laptop as it is so damn true to life.

Online dating can be awesome but overwhelming at the same time and it can be hard to keep with the same standards you would use in real life. I can suggest being a little pickier during the whole vetting phase and following your intuition more so with the head and not the heart as you have not met that person yet and so it should in theory be easier to dismiss them.

I did make a list of the desired qualities/attributes that mattered to me. When I say list, it was a couple of things not even worthy of being called a list. Fun, witty with a dry sense of humour and a fantastic bum was not a big ask, well, at least I did not think so.

Saying that, I learnt not to be too dismissive, or I would have a new issue of deleting an 'expression of interest' because of something that could be overlooked in real life but happened to be on a profile.

In the weird and wonderful world of internet dating, most of the time it's been more weird than wonderful, there are certain types of individuals one would come across.

These individuals that I am categorising are based upon my own personal experiences in the seven years, yes seven years that I have been single and am still searching for the elusive one.

We may all be accused of chasing unicorns but we are obsessed with the magic, fantasy, romance, call it what you will, of the unicorn being out there, grazing peacefully whilst waiting for us to approach and calmly take the initiative and whisper sweet nothings or anything we deem charming in to its ear and then sling on the reigns and tame the beast!

Most of the time though, we do come across mares, jackasses and donkeys such as the types of people I am going to be categorising and will be highlighted later on. Granted I am highlighting observations from the male perspective but the categories can be attributed to both sexes and any race, creed or colour.

The lines quoted in the scenarios are frequently used as a result of basically what happens in near enough nine times out of ten. In fact, it happens so often it's quite scary almost being able to guess what the other person is about to say.

So... what are these categories you may be wondering? Well, they are bit like the following.

1) *The Ghost*

The ghost is an entity that somehow manages to log onto a computer set up a profile, then contact you and subsequently disappear! Poof!

Many websites have both industry common and their own unique ways of types of communication.

Some have a 'wave' or 'expression of interest' button, which consists of sending the lady you are interested in a wave or expression of interest just to test the water and see if you get one back.

If you do get a 'wave' back, then 'fun times' ahead! Well... maybe, let's not get carried away yet and start planning the names of our unborn children! Then we send a message using the internal email system of the site and hope they respond. Nothing.

You may not get anything back but they have read the message and seen your profile – some websites have that functionality to enable you to ascertain that also. Some even have a feature a bit like whatsapp, the date and time of email being read and even the infamous twin blue ticks!

There are times when the lady may actually contact you with the bonus being she has a profile pic! And she's hot too! whoop! whoop!

You then send her an email with contact details and see what happens. Nothing. She has seen your email, on the day you sent it even, but nothing.

You send another one a week later pretending that you had IT issues and you are not sure if she received the email sent on a prior occasion (trying to play it cool) hence why you are sending another one now. Nothing. She received it. She read it. She ignored it.

Maybe it was not a real female but the spirit or ghost of dates of past! But somehow, it all seemed so real or was it?

2) Not Quite Over the Ex

There is nothing anyone can do about this individual. Things could be going along great for three months, in terms of texting every day whether it be a simple 'Good Morning & hope you have a fab day' or a full blown conversation in between morning coffees and meetings at work, catch up chit chat on the phone every couple of days in the evening and meeting up at least once or twice a week. Promising stuff!

Then Bam! You will receive a text/phone call out of the blue that goes a bit like "Look (insert name), I have something important on my mind to tell you". The fact that the potential significant other has used your name, not nickname or pet name bestowed upon thee since you both decided to 'officially' start dating is a clue in itself.

The next line will be something like, *"Well….. I have just received a phone call/text/email from my ex- boyfriend/ fiancé/husband… and… erm… I'm not sure what to do."*

'Here we go again' enters one's mind and then we start thinking, *'Damn, I really like this girl but I'm not going to play second fiddle to anyone! How do I word this without coming across as an idiot whilst being firm but fair? I don't want to drive her into the arms of the ex but I don't want to come across as clingy and desperate, even though I am the latter!'*

Ok, here goes, I then come out with the following, *"Well, what can I say? You're not getting a threesome out of this!"* (I try to add humour to the downplay the tension I am feeling whilst making me look cool and hope that makes her divert her decision towards me me me!)

I quickly then add the line *"Look, I'll tell you what… take some time out to think about it… only you can make the decision on what to do and where it goes from here… and I shall wait to hear from you in a week… how does that grab you?"*

Nine times out of ten, I never hear from her again!

3) Miss IDK (I don't know)

There is being indecisive on some things, and then there is being so indecisive on everything to a point you dare not ask that indecisive person anything at all.

Life is complicated and busy enough that we don't have time to figure out what they may want or mean or may not want or mean.

When finally agreeing upon a time, date and location for a first date after much indecisiveness, there is the awkward silence in between questions. Rather than a flowing conversation between the two of us, as one would expect it to be, it becomes more like an interview/Q&A session.

Q: So…..how are you finding the world of internet dating?
A: Uhm… dunno

Q: What made you join the website or want to try internet dating?
A: Erm… I don't know really

Q: What type of guy do you generally go for?
A: Don't know, I'm not sure

Q: Are you after a serious relationship or casual?
A: Err… dunno

Q: Would you like tea or coffee?
A: Ooohh… I don't know

And so it goes on and on… surprisingly at the end of the date she comes out with the *'it was really nice chatting to you'* comment. Hmmm… Strange, I only remember there being talking on my part and that was from asking the questions just to initiate some form of conversation!

4) The Dictator/Miss Tyrant

What can I say about this type of person? This person will take the meaning of perfectionist to another level. Perfection being her standard or calibre but not necessarily the one attributable to what may be considered by the general population as the norm.

If you were to mention anything about your personality or hobbies as per normal, then take a deep breath and behold the onslaught of rules about to be issued.

"If you want to be with me, you will be doing… more often."

"There is no way I would let you keep on doing… when we get together/ engaged/ married."

"Why do you spend your money on that? What a waste! I think we shall put a stop to… don't you agree it's for the best?"

It's all about compromise, AKA do what she wants and the way she wants it and then all will be well with the world and woe betide anyone who dare to deviate!

Experience has taught me to look out for the key lines as detailed above and avoid as soon as one of the said key lines is spoken.

5) *The Window Shopper*

Ah yes! These are the heartbreakers I am afraid. Like with the ladies who are not quite over their Ex, the texts, phone calls and meet ups are regular and like clockwork even.

The only difference here is the time period you are 'in communication' with each other unless you have mutually agreed that you are dating.

These ladies have no intention of being with someone or settling down, well… at least with me anyhow.

They like to see if they 'still have it' and like to know what they can attract but when it comes to the phase of getting serious i.e. possible discussion on maybe exclusively dating each other only and seeing where it goes, then prepare to get ghosted or broken up with.

I personally have come across a lot of these Window Shoppers on my dating adventures. No tell-tale signs for these I'm afraid, when it happens it happens.

6) *Must Do Better*

This category follows on nicely from the Window Shopper. They are almost the same type of person but the difference here is the lady wants to climb the 'dating ladder' and get that trophy husband/boyfriend/partner.

With the exception of knowing she must climb the dating ladder, this lady can't make her own decisions and will need to obtain approval from all of her family and friends (past and present and those random strangers connected with from LinkedIn and Facebook) to see if you are up to standard before even contemplating going on a date with you.

This means, she will like telling her friends, family etc. about the guy she is 'kind of seeing'* and then likes to reel off the stats accordingly.

"Well everyone… the guy I am 'kind of seeing' is called… and he is a (doctor/ lawyer/ accountant etc.) who drives a (BMW/ Mercedes, etc.) who lives in (Birmingham/Edinburgh) and wears nothing but designer clothing and holidays at least once every three months albeit city breaks in Europe and wants to take me too… etc."

*'Kind of seeing'** is safer than saying dating. Dating implies that she has made up her mind and is going to settle for and down with this one. It's too serious, it's too onerous, it's too much pressure!

Then, before you know it, this poor guy will get dropped and ghosted as a better one (deal or spec) comes along. I like using car analogies as you can tell.

"Well everyone, the last guy wasn't really the type that I go for so I dumped him yesterday – don't want to talk about it,

but… the guy I am now 'kind of seeing' is called … and he is a (plastic surgeon/judge/financial director or CEO, etc.) who drives a (Ferrari/Porsche/Lambo/Range Rover, etc.) who lives in (London/New York, etc.) and wears nothing but Saville Row and holidays at least once a month every month somewhere far flung by private jet and wants to take me too… etc."

These people cannot be helped and are hard to avoid unless you have managed to figure them out initially. The figuring them out is the hardest part.

7) *The Juggler*

OMG! At one stage of our lives we may all be guilty of having done this. Dating or meeting up with too many potentials! It's a juggling act!

It can be great fun or a complete disaster! It can be both from the point of view of The Juggler or the one being juggled.

I shall use a bus analogy to describe this one.

Getting interests and dates are a bit like catching a bus. You wait around for ages, nothing. Then suddenly two or three of them come along at once and you don't know which one to catch!

They all look nice and shiny and comfortable and well worth the ride! erm… I mean the wait!

However, there are those rare moments when you have enough busses to fill a depot! A whole fleet to choose from and admire! Naturally, one can be taken aback and overwhelmed and not know which one to 'test drive' first!

Naturally, we don't want to waste time and accidentally choose the one that is expensive to run, high maintenance and quite temperamental either! Or do we go for the one with a few more miles on the clock but not quite a banger but is comfortable and reliable?

What does one do? We date and meet up with all of them! Try and whittle it down to a couple and then ultimately the one.

The fun begins. We mix up the names, the hobbies, the professions, the history and generally everything and repeat conversations, one liners and jokes thinking they are original and don't tell them to the ones who have not heard them, etc.

It becomes a real mess. On the other hand, some can juggle numerous people and whittle down accordingly and really show a knack of remembering the details and thus is not a problem.

8) The Experimenter

Now admittedly, I have only ever encountered this type of female when I have ascertained that I am not the 'normal' type of guy she would date. I was fortunate enough to have these ladies tell me so, hence the category.

I would have to relay some personal experiences in further detail in order to emphasise this one.

In one case, it transpired I was the only guy a certain lady had dated in the space of a couple of years. This was only as she was now getting bored of women! She then met another girl on a work's night out a couple of weeks later and that was that, but interesting as an experience though. Damn, was dating me enough to make her go off men completely? I guess I will never know.

Another case, happened to be a Caucasian lady of Irish heritage. There were not many Indian men in the part of Ireland where she hailed from and thus she wanted to *"see what you lot are like"*.

Wow! So it wasn't my funny profile or picture then? Seems like I was going to be representing British Asian men whether I liked it or not and felt pressured not to disappoint!

Occasionally I have come across ladies who just want to rebel and date someone their dad may not approve of. I tend to just roll with it and enjoy the ride until it ends.

Fortunately, these cases have seldom happened in my experience but felt it worth mentioning as they were very much memorable not to be excluded.

9) The Inbetweener

I don't intend to besmirch one of my favourite TV shows of all time with this description but it is the only way I can describe the next category.

For the record I am also guilty of this myself. I have been someone's Inbetweener and made someone mine also.

The Inbetweener is someone whom you may have stumbled across after a dry patch on the dating scene.

Picture the scenario. You are bored at home one evening and there is nothing on TV to watch, no shows to binge watch, you've been to the gym, all of your friends have plans with their families or other social circles and you are just plain bored.

What is else is there to do? Check my personal emails and kill a bit of time by seeing what is left on the dating sites of course! Check the profiles of those that you have not dated or has not blatantly rejected your expression of interest. Lo and behold! There are some new profiles that have recently joined! There is a slight issue though. None of them pop out at you like the prior profiles that led to dates of past.

Your initial thoughts *are "Hmmm, maybe. Not sure about this one. Dunno. Ah hell, let's just send out an expression and see what she says. It won't matter much as I'm not really feeling it but it'll be a nice surprise if anything happens!"*

The only issue here is, I have done this with ten others! What has just happened is a mail shot has been sent in essence. The Inbetweener's normally pop up after the mailshot has been sent out and next thing you know I have become a Juggler!

It is a tad cruel but, you know there is not much about the person but the fear of being lonely creeps in. You go on dates and have phone calls but still not much. Nothing wrong with the person but there is no spark or chemistry or anything. You feel a tad guilty and then relieved when she starts ghosting you as you then know she has met someone else. Phew!

10) The Chancer

There are some that just didn't bother to read your profile and will be the complete opposite to what you want. They took a chance in case you said *"hmmm… yes… okay!"* I mean 'really?!'

Being UK born and bred, with reference to Indian dating sites, and clearly stating I am only interested in UK pro-files, I have now gained an international following in Toronto, Chandigarh and more recently Kuala Lumpur.

Chances are, if I were to pack up and leave to go and live amongst the 'fans', then the popularity would dissipate and a new fan club would form in Birmingham.

Granted, there are probably a few more categories that can be added, such as Stalker and Clingy, etc. but then that may be too many.

11) The Casting Agent

There are some who are not happy with the pictures that you have on your profile. If you only had the one, albeit fantastic, then it's understandable. If you have at least five or six then it should suffice. Right? Wrong! Not in their eyes. It does not matter if they initiate contact with you or vice versa, you need to have a professional portfolio at the ready.

I am talking a set of ten with just poses in monotone. Another set of ten photos on a recent holiday. Another set of ten doing an activity to prove you actually do what is stated in the profile. Yes you will be screwed if you had lied and mentioned flying helicopters!

Even then it's still not enough! They want the same picture but from numerous angles that even David Bailey would struggle with!

12) Self-Proclaimed Miss Wonderful

There is a song by The Proclaimers – I'm Gonna Be (500 miles) with a catchy chorus declaring a willingness to walk 500 miles.

I think of this song whenever I encounter this type of women, but for these specimens, I don't even want to walk 500 paces.

I like many others love a sassy, vibrant, confident woman. Who doesn't? Then sometimes you stumble across Miss Wonderful.

I am all for loving and respecting one's self and appreciating self-worth, then there are times when the fine line between confidence and arrogance becomes a huge blur of a line that was painted using a roller!

Would it not be better to say *"Others have described me as being... and also..."*, or even be the one to bestow the praises upon her and have her blush upon receipt of many compliments? The humble and unaware they are, the more I want to compliment them and relish making them feel special and wanted, even if things do not work out romantically.

Instead, it's rather more a case of:

"I am extremely funny, sexy with it, down to earth, grounded, beautiful, fun to be around, vibrant and exciting to be with, enrich lives of those around me and I happen to be very selective of those I let into my life and any man would be fortunate with me. I only go for manly guys with bulging biceps and who are over 6ft."

Ladies and gentlemen, I bullshit thee not. This is an actual profile of one of the girls who expressed an interest in me. I honestly could not believe what I was reading.

I really had to supress the urge to respond back with:

"Hi there, wow! There are three things I despise in life. The first being lists. The second being modesty. The final one being irony! If I were indeed to be the lucky one to even breathe the same air as you on a date, then surely I would be the one you from whom you would have received the compliments on your character? Anyhow, on this occasion, I am not seeing anyone and will not keep your profile on file for future reference in case I get desperate and change my mind. Good luck as you may need it!"

After a journey of discovery, I have found that I am quite fond of clingy ladies. It's nice being wanted. In fact the clingier the better! The only issue is, I find, they turn into Tyrants after a short while hence why the dating/relationships have not lasted long.

I even had a stalker for a short while. Now, to be honest, initially, I was amused, bemused and astonished that someone would devote time and effort to stalk me. It was flattering even.

Yes okay the calls at silly o'clock in the early hours of the morning were a tad inconvenient but hey, that's why we have silent mode on mobile phones right? I was not sure whether to be relieved or offended when the stalking ceased after two and a half weeks. Two and a half weeks! I mean is that it?! Is that all I am worth?! Could she not be arsed to carry on until at least the end of the month?! Round it up to whole numbers?!

This is next stage after having received a message and pre meeting up. You are being judged. Will you be nervous and sound like Joe Pasquale and get on her nerves, or try and adopt a form of well spoken twang and talk like Harry Enfield in *Kevin and Perry Go Large*!

I always recall a Michael McIntyre sketch highlighting Northern folk who would have moved to London and suddenly their accent changes.

From my own experiences, I too have encountered those fair maidens who would ask "How can I compare thee to a summer's day?" like a Charlotte Bronte English Rose on the phone, and then upon meeting them, the fair maiden becomes a Waynetta Tavern Wench of Olde and asks "Yaum alright bab"!

We digress. Or rather I do. Anyhow, let us say the telephone call with the fair maiden of choice is due this evening at six for example.

The drive on the way home from work will be *"What do I say to her? How shall I start the conversation other than using the word Hello? I know! I shall use Bongiorno! What if she is fluent in Italian? She likes to travel and she wants a funny guy and not just funny looking either! Shit!! I'm screwed again!"*

Granted we probably all don't do that but sometimes we do come across that golden nugget of a profile and basically we don't want to cock it up and look stupid and not even have her agree to a date before we even get started!

The Telephone Interview

Right, let's say we are fast approaching six o'clock. What do we do? Do we call on the dot and give the possible impression we are desperate or very keen? Or do we call at half past six and then come across as too relaxed or even not bothered about keeping them waiting with our poor timekeeping?

I might be accused of thinking too deep into these things but upon conversing with many a friend and colleague on the subject of dating and other attributes associated, it is apparent that the initial conversation will set the tone and direction of whatever may be going forwards.

Okay, it's ten past six! Ring Ring Ring baby! WTF?! Damn her phone is engaged! Ok, no problem, we shall call back in a few.

It's now a quarter past six. Okay, deep breaths! In… and now out… don't give birth to anything! Okay Ring Ring Ring! Shit not again! It's gone through to voicemail! Damn it. Shall I leave a voice message? Sod it. Let's.

You feel like saying:

"Hi… it's me. You know, the guy whom you asked to call you at six o'clock! You were engaged and now not answering. Buzz me back if you're serious as I have plenty of other shit to do this evening. Bye!"

But actually, what you end up saying, in a cool and calm manner, would put any diplomat to shame:

"Hi… It's me! Just calling to see how you're doing. It looks like I have just missed you. No problemo. I hope all is okay and I shall catch up with you as and when. Take Care. Bye!"

As soon as the phone is hung up, a number of thoughts will enter the mind.

"Hopefully it's not the flirt divert number and some dodgy DJ will not be playing it on the radio for all to hear and ridicule!"

"Will she actually bother to answer back? What if she has no reception? Why wouldn't she? She agreed to the phone call?"

Then a stroke of pure genius! I shall send her a whatsapp! Brilliant! I basically then put the same sentence down into words on whatsapp and send. I then proceed to do the hokey cokey with whatsapp. I'm logged in. I'm logged out. In. Out. In. Out. Shake the phone about!

"Whoah! She is online! She has received the message as there are now two ticks! They're blue! Hallelujah! Hallelujah! Halle Lujah! Eh? WTF?! She has logged out! God damn!"

Wait a minute, wait a minute! The phone buzzes and then the Benny Hill ring tone starts to blare out! Louder and louder and building to a crescendo!

One ring – nope, too early, too desperate!

Two rings – nope, still too early!

Three rings – not yet, steady on fella! Just one more!

Four rings – quick! Pick up pick up you damn fool before it goes to voicemail

Then I answer the phone cool, calm and collected.

"Bonjour! (I go French)*, comon ca'va ce soir? How are we? … What was I doing? … Oh nothing much. Just pottering around and lost track of time."* Yes people. Cool and calm bullshit at its best.

The next part is nothing I can control. The profile may say one thing but she may be the same person or a complete loon. I always have to play it by ear on these and adlib accordingly.

Fortunately, I would have been like a plastic mould machine and made a great impression and thus, as a result, managed to organise a date or meet up dependant on home and work life schedules.

Types of Dates

Happy Coincidence Dates

Well... did I get really bad or great memorable dates from these sites? Of course I did. In fact I have lost count of how many. These encounters of the third kind have defined my approach to dating and helped educate me on myself and help ascertain what I would like and do not want from a relationship and partner. Luckily for me there was no exam as I would have failed abysmally.

I discovered great restaurants, coffee houses and bars in other towns and cities as well as the ones that I knew existed in my home city but never really had a reason to go to them in the past. As a result, I now frequent them regularly with family and friends as well as with other dates.

Routine Dates

Don't get me wrong, I am all for spontaneity. It's a Gemini trait and I like to keep things fresh and interesting and can get bored of routine. Sometimes dates have been like that. Very routine.

They can be a routine with the only difference being the lady. The time, venue, night of the week and even the bar staff have been the same on occasion. It has all been dependent on the choice of lady and by sheer coincidence the times are similar and the location just happens to be the latest place to be. Then on the flipside, if I happen to be at a particular place on a certain night of the week, it's just easier to stick to the same and make for an easier compare and contrast session afterwards.

I have been the recipient of the wry smile or cheeky grin from the barista on many an occasion. No words are spoken but line that could be spoken almost telepathically is the same:

"Ah it's you again! Good evening. Another lovely lady in tow I see. Wow! My word! You really are punching above your weight with this one! Well, good luck with this one and if not, I shall see you next week at the same time. Enjoy!"

Routine means I have found it easier to try and impress the lady with the knowledge of the menu also. Normal conversation then tends to be:

Me: *I can really recommend the hot chocolate with cinnamon rolls here.*

Lady: *Oh really? Why? Have you tried everything on the menu then?*

Me: *Oh no, my first time here. I have heard great things about this place and thought it was worth checking out and hoped you would like it, what do you think so far?*

This gave me time to see what she would come out with and try and imagine what it would be like to kiss her.

A good friend of mine once told me never imagine yourself married to the person you are meeting. That is asking for disaster. Too many preconceptions. Too much pressure and fault finding follows. It's easier to just imagine kissing them and then checking out a favourite body part, subtly, and then taking it from there.

Invite Yourself to Dinner Why Don't You?

The discovery of restaurants has been down to dates inviting themselves to dinner. Whether they had meant to or not I shall never know and I am past the point of trying it figure it all out.

On many occasions I have had to meet up after work and even squeeze in a quick one, a date that is, between meeting up with friends later on that evening. Unless, a scene from Hollywood is being re-enacted, I never expect to go back to theirs for a 'coffee'. Normally it's an hour or so and then decide on the way home or to my next venue of choice if it's marry, snog or avoid.

If I am meeting up with a date and have plans later on then, like most, and as one would expect, I let them know that I have plans later on that evening so that they won't get offended or rushed. Most first dates in my experience are only an hour or so anyhow.

However, once in a while, a golden nugget of a date pops along. She doesn't care about my plans for the evening! Oh no no no! She will be gone when she is done with the Q&A session and has had enough!

To make things worse, she then orders food. Granted, six o'clock maybe a dinner time for some so naturally I will also indulge in a starter so as not to make her feel left out and to keep my strength up and provide sustenance if the date is hard going.

The WTF moment is when she decides to order mains and then hands me the menu and looks expectantly at me and decides to judge me by my choice. I say WTF moment as she will have been aware that I am planning on meeting up with friends for a meal later on that evening.

I would have even told her this before meeting up on the phone just so it was not a lastminute.com surprise!

This is when I start to start to consume the foods with the dreaded 'S' word.

Salads! I hate salads with a passion. I am a gym bunny and hit it hard when I train and have been told I have a good physique at 6ft3 and nearly 15 stone trying to get to a 10% body fat (just thought I would throw that in). I eat plenty of fruit and vegetables and am a carnivore but hate salads with a passion. The only time I will eat anything that resembles salad is when it happens to be in a Burger

King Whopper on a cheat day. End of. Soggy, wet, green tasteless waste of time. Rant over.

The icing on the cake is literally when she orders a cake or a pudding or a desert with icing! I've tried to eat the smallest and lightest dishes the restaurant will have on the menu just so that I am able to enjoy my meal and company later on that evening.

I am too polite to embarrass the lady, especially in front of the waitress, by saying *"Look, I cannot eat anything as I told you when organising this meet up that I have a meal with friends later on this evening."* Call me gutless or soppy but I feel it ruins the mood somewhat. Hence why I only ever have a starter or just try and avoid dates on the same day/evening as other social functions. Lesson learnt.

What Days and Who Pays?

Talking of food, the contentious point that should not come up but does generate passion in a conversation amongst friends is that of the bill and who should pick up the tab.

Call me old fashioned, but...... I do believe in picking up the tab especially if I have asked that person out on a date. Coffee shop first date? Then most definitely the guy should pay. It's only going to cost an afternoon of the guy's time and realistically, the money involved is minimal unless the gentleman invited the lady to Afternoon Cream Tea at Claridges in London. Then he is screwed if he were to try to impress and go above his societal status and budget.

On the outside he would say *"Oh yes, you cannot beat an English Cream Tea. I love to pop in every week and have a cup of soothing, refreshing cha! With a slice of homemade cake!"*

On the inside it may be more a case of *"WTF! How much? I could buy a kettle for the price of the tea alone! How on earth did they calculate the price of the cake?! Cost plus 1000%? I could buy a bakery and bake my own!"*

I have heard many friends and colleagues recount their stories of trying to impress the fairer sex and then feeling embarrassed to ask the lady to contribute due to underestimating the prices.

In my experience, the first date has always been a coffee if on a weekend and a wine bar if on a weeknight. I have been advised by a couple of my close female friends never to encroach on a ladies evening. Best advice I have ever received on women.

Therefore, the first dates that have been on a weekend always take place in an afternoon, hence a coffee shop. A nice relaxed atmosphere and no pressure for both parties to look superhot as they would initially try to if it were an evening date. The plus side is we get to see each other when we are most relaxed and looking casual. The normal everyday look.

Just in case the first date happens to be a harrowing experience, then the lady in question has the evening to recuperate with friends and can either wallow in a sea of despair or move on and be thankful.

If the date happened to be a pleasant one, then at least the lady can decide whether to devote her next Friday or Saturday to me in case there is a second date. If a second date is on the cards and happens to be in an evening, then the opportunity is rife to impress and blow their minds with my lack of dress sense! Absolutely epic!

I have even highlighted and emphasised to my dates that I do not wish to encroach upon their evening plans with family or friends. I then come across as considerate and accommodating which can only win brownie points.

When the second date comes round, the venue depends on the how good a relationship I have built up with my date. If she is still distant then it can just be drinks, if she and I are more comfortable then it can be a meal beforehand or afterwards. Even then, I pick up the tab accordingly.

I have had the experience of meeting up with a certain female from Telford at least five times and go for meals and then have her not offer to participate towards it.

On these occasions, I have sat there taking what may seem an age, but entirely intentional, to retrieve my wallet from my pocket whilst smiling but watching the face of my date for any sign of movement.

By movement, I mean watching the lips move and hearing her say the words, *"Hey, look, why don't we split the bill?"* even if not with the conviction of sincerity.

Realistically, I would not have accepted the offer to go Dutch but the thought and offer is always appreciated. Most guys I have spoken to about this have echoed the same thoughts.

Instead, I watch the lack of eye contact being made and the iPhone being flipped out to check a message from a guy that she ignored texts from a month or so ago but now feels the need to respond and pretend she is busy. Then a frown appears on her face, she purses her lips and then shakes her head and makes a tut tut sound. It's a way of saying, *"Don't disturb me, I am so stressed out right now, nothing is going right today!"* without saying it.

Strangely enough, the smile re-emerges when my card is extracted from my wallet and placed slowly but gently on to the leather wallet or fake silver tray that has the bill laid upon it.

The phone is strewn back into the Mary Poppins size bag immediately and thus a new conversation may begin.

There are some ladies who will just be blatant and tell me that they are old-fashioned and expect the guy to pay. End of. At least you know where you stand with them.

I do feel like saying *"Despite being Indian, I've never been to Nando's! Let's go there for our next date!"* just to get a reaction over a cheaper date. Surely my company is more important than the menu choice?

Yeah right, as if she will jump around in her chair and have her eyes light up brightly and say *"No, even better, let's do KFC! It's finger licking good and I am a fan of Colonel Sanders!"*

Now for another contentious point on which there is no doubt that many will disagree. Based on my personal experiences, it has been predominantly the Indian ladies who will just expect and accept the guy paying for everything all the time, every time. The non-Indian ladies tend to be those who will either buy the next round of drinks or go Dutch on the meal.

Regardless of what nationality or ethnic origin or woman I am dating, it's hard to judge on these things. The last thing I wanted to do is come across as a tight-arsed accountant. Being frugal can be a huge put off. My only advice to myself is to know my date.

If I knew them, then I wouldn't still be single!

Speed Dating Time!

If online dating isn't for you there are always obvious alternatives like heading to places with like-minded people, hanging out with friends, and talking to everyone you meet.

Nowadays, I'm an advocate of talking crap to whoever's sitting next to me at a bar. There is always uncertainty with regards to whom you will encounter on that occasion but you never know when you'll make a new friend through networking for a partner.

I have even utilised my skill of being able to do accents to a great extent so as to pretend I am a stranger in town and require advice on the best places to visit and as a result get asked to tag along. Result!

However, I don't recommend this as it can get awkward when you bump in to the same group of ladies the following week whilst chatting to a new encounter, and you are no longer a Glaswegian tambourine repair man but a South African Car salesman on this occasion! Honesty is the best policy of course.

We don't all have time to frequent a wine bar or club every night, but the quest to find a new hobby ensues so as to find like-minded individuals.

The nice thing about meeting people in real life is that you're typically friends first, so you've already got plenty to talk about.

Let's say for arguments sake, we lived in a dystopian world and there is a worldwide mandatory law or requirement for all members of society to undertake a personality test and be attributed a coloured badge that had to be worn at all times. For example, Yellow badge indicates fun, lively and spirited. Grey indicated boring, reserved and introverted, a bit like Virgo females. Just kidding.

Let's also say that we had to be 'single' if we were to frequent a 'singles' bar', 'singles event' or just plainly wanted to flirt. Thus far, everything is black and white. Now, we often hear people talking about how much personality is key and looks are not. Load of bullshit. We all know it but somehow hold on to the glimmer of hope that maybe, just maybe, the person whom we are interested in forgot what we looked like and only remembered the personality.

Naturally there has to be an attraction but unless the person expressing an interest interacts on a daily basis with their person of choice, in a bar or outside of work as strangers, nothing is going to happen.

At these types of events there is normally an occasion to mingle either beforehand or afterwards and quite often, one is presented an opportunity to 'check out the goods' and also 'check out the competition'. It becomes a normal night out in a bar or club after the event has taken place and it's the only chance to 'sell yourself' as the participants will have no choice but to talk to you albeit for three minutes or so.

Speed Dating Indian vs Western

My close friend David, with whom I had formulated the quote on trying to figure out women, met his Indian wife at a non-Indian speed dating event. I even recall having to almost beg him to come along earlier on that evening as he was getting bored of it all. Luckily for him he did.

Certain dating websites have speed date events and/or padlock parties. For those of you who have a free weeknight or two and fancy doing something different, this is a must.

You can have as much fun as you want if you approach with an open mind and no inhibitions.

Whoever said be yourself had no idea what they were talking about – lie lie lie and be whomever you want to be! Chances are, you will not see these people again! Ever!

I personally have noticed such a huge difference when attending the Indian ones compared to the non-Indian events.

I have turned up to an Indian speed dating event and instantly greeted the organiser with a "Hello! I am here for a wife, in Punjabi we call it a wehffe!" It can go either of two ways. The organiser can laugh with me or give me the weirdest look and the participants who have arrived earlier then look at me and think 'avoid'! Fun times ahead!

I can turn up to a non-Indian event and greet the organiser with a put on broad Brummie or Midlands accent that the likes of Ozzy Osbourne, UB40, Duran Duran and Nigel Mansell could be proud of and ask "Can yaum guarantee I'll pull a bird on this fing tonight mate?"

The thing is, although participants are advised to take the speed date seriously, many don't. For me, I have found a light hearted/softer approach tends to work best. Don't expect to find your future spouse at one of these!

On the Indian events, if the same group of single people that constantly attend these events have not arrived then it can be fun to watch. I have found the build up to the event mesmerising to watch. I enjoy people watching to a point, i.e. whilst waiting for a friends in a bar or restaurant. The speed dating experience is in the same boat.

The Indian girls arrive in twos or threes and thus hang in those clumps generally. The ones who arrived by themselves tend to seek out other members of the sisterhood of Singleville who have also arrived solo. They then tend to bond and eye up the males who have arrived thus far. Pretty normal stuff.

The Indian guys on the other hand have flown in solo. They give each other male in the venue a nod of brotherly solidarity but won't really strike up the Bromance as technically the other man is the competition. The ones who are confident will try and mingle beforehand with the fairer sex and ascertain whom is worth the three-minute time limit and one liners and who is not.

The male pharmacists are a tad petrified. I have noticed they will sit there and interact with no one. They will slowly try and dissect and push around the ice in their orange juice or coke rather than interact with anyone at all.

I'm not saying we accountants are pickup artists but due to the fact we tend to get given a rough ride for being boring, we at least try not to conform to the stereotype and strike up a conversation with the barmaid and seen what the score is. I tend to ask how the events have gone in the past generally and take it from there. If I play my cards right I end up getting her number instead if the choice at speed dating is limited.

In my experience, the Indian girls, most of the time, are at the events to kill time. Their cousins/university friends are over for the weekend and they want to kill a bit of time before they have to get to the pre-booked restaurant meal later on in the evening and then hitting a club at the end.

The Indian guys are dismayed when the ladies tend to leave early for the evening to either go home/go to the restaurant or on to another venue without the guys they have just encountered in tow. Poor fellows, this was their time! They thought they had met the one! They wished their mum was here to see her! She may have approved! The same old pattern emerges every time. Hence why I have stopped going to the Indian ones initially as they didn't quite get dry humour.

The non-Indian ladies tend to be more open and up for a good evening. So what if they did not find their potential partner tonight? They had a great time and made some good friends, male and female and a potential new social group.

As a result of forming a new social group from having attended one of these events, we then proceeded to organise a few nights out and attend other speed dating events and padlock parties subsequently. It was a win–win situation.

The non-Indian guys are like the Indian guys in terms of having arrived solo. These guys have a lot more confidence I have noticed. Not only will you get a nod of brotherly solidarity but Bromance will be struck up. Therefore, another social circle formed! Whether it be Bromance or romance, everyone seems more chilled and has a great time.

I have then reached a point in the evening where the three minutes allocated seem like an eternity and I wish I could grab the whistle used by the organiser and blow it myself or next time just bring my own. Sod's Law they may use a bell instead on the next one!

What makes its tricky is trying to remember the number the of the lady I had just spoken to and to write a form of code or something short that will make sense later on whilst trying to make my way to the next victim, I mean lady, in a booth, and juggle a drink without tripping, slipping or spilling it.

Occasionally we come across the 'One word wonder woman' on these occasions. She will be the type who is disinterested in both you and the whole experience. Aloof in fact and will as her title suggests only answer with one word.

This may sound cruel but it is time to have fun and enjoy the evening and not let this person put a dampener on the whole experience. I could go down one of two routes or both.

Route One: Be suggestive but don't act like a sleaze. This comes naturally to most men but with there being a push more towards the sleazy side.

I used to ask question such as what her porn star name would be. The first name being your pet's name and the surname being your mother's maiden name tends to be the rule. This usually grabs the attention and stops the one word answers.

Route Two: Lie about myself and my profession completely. It can work especially if the person is not my type and I have no interest in seeing her again after the three minutes expire.

The Lie: I am a yacht broker. So I bamboozle her with manufacturers of these majestic off-shore cruisers such as *Princess*, *Sealine*, *Huntsman*, *Pershing*, *Sunseeker*, etc. just to show I know my stuff in case she googles any of them. One girl did in fact do just that in front of me!

I then drop nautical puns into the conversation and see if she gets any of them. Some do and appreciate them, many don't. In fact I was so proud of my nautical puns I actually wrote a profile for one of my friends who actually enjoyed sailing regularly being on a boat. She was grateful but didn't receive attention from whom she wanted.

Two-Faced or Multidimensional?

There have times when I, like many others I hope, have been wondering what am I doing wrong? Why is it not happening? I'm a blooming catch damn it!

I exclaimed this to a work colleague and friend of mine who immediately knew the score. She was instrumental in helping me whittle down profiles and choose 'more appropriate ones'.

The thing is, she was very interested in astrology and horoscopes and palmistry to a point. I'm not a sceptic, but it wasn't a field I was particularly interested in and even knew much about.

The fact I am a Gemini male made a lot of difference in terms of whom I should be 'concentrating' on and whom I should just avoid completely.

Now, I must clarify that my first line to a potential lady is not "Hi, Gemini male! Pleased to meet you, what sign are you baby?!" But, fortunately some of the dating websites used would divulge such details, especially the Indian ones.

The good thing is this detail became a bit of a tool in helping to narrow down profiles. Not only did it help to stimulate the mind, it helped raise my game in terms of formulating ways of dropping in my star sign and then trying to ascertain the star sign through normal conversation. Quite tricky! There were epic fails at times.

Indian and Non-Indian ladies would respond with "Why are you asking me that?"

Non-Indian ladies would follow that by 'Okay… Are you a fan of Mystic Meg or something you weirdo?!" and then try and laugh it off.

The Indian ladies caught on to it straight away like flies to dog turd. They would respond with "Blimey!…..You're keen!"

Ordinarily, Sikh and Hindu families that I know have some belief in the astrology and the stars and would consult someone with expertise in this field like a Pandat (Temple Priest) and divulge the star signs of potential pairings whilst showing him a photo of the currently happy couple. The priest would either then say yes or hell no!

Anyhow, my friend, who is an English rose, had even made a list of the ladies I should only be interested in. I was to avoid Capricorn, Scorpio, Virgo, Taurus and fellow Geminis too! This was 42% of the potentials out there!

Like a true friend would, I ignored her and carried on anyhow. I suppose like many men, I was and still am a sucker for a pretty woman. I can't help it.

It was only when the relationships did not work out and ended a lot sooner than I would have liked or just did not take off, I then took a step back and evaluated. My friend was right all along!

Now, I hasten to add the interactions and evaluations are based purely on my own experiences and, although may come across as sweeping generalisations, are not intended to be.

Gemini Man and Taurus Lady – I did not date too many of these but on all occasions I found these ladies too boring. They were never into anything I was. I know people mention opposites attract but there were too many in this case.

Gemini Man and Virgo Lady – Forget it. Too much of a perfectionist and constantly fussing and nagging. These Ice Maidens will mess around and be too distant and aloof! You will never know where you stand with these and their self-preservation kicks in a lot harsher than mutual consideration for both parties and feelings.

Gemini Man and Capricorn Lady – Very fickle in my experience. Thought of themselves very highly and nothing or anyone was good enough for them. The very few of these I dated turned out to be exactly the same.

Gemini Man and Scorpio Lady – Wow! Whirlwind relationships every time with these ladies but not in a good way. Constant mind games and drama but they are so damn hot! I knew they were wrong but lust took over. Glutton for punishment would keep going back for more and then get stung, and stung hard!

Gemini Man and Gemini Lady – The ex-wife was a Gemini. We even had the same birthday so I couldn't really forget it. I did try and avoid but now and again a golden nugget popped up and I had to indulge. Couldn't resist!

Now I am not saying that I only date the ladies in that 'most compatible' camp, as now and again I do stumble across a golden nugget, but I when I get that *'umm… erm… I don't know… nah! Forget about it'* kind of feeling then knowing the star sign has helped.

Whether that approach has hindered my ability to find 'the one' I will not know for sure. However, the relationships I have had subsequently have tended to be more pleasant and involved more amicable break ups with less drama than when I was in relationships with the 'least compatible' star sign.

Gemini men are not perfect but almost there! I jest of course. We are multidimensional and not two-faced. We can adapt accordingly in many situations and groups of people and feel the need to be stimulated and not bored. We can get bored very easily. We just happen to be youthful, chilled out and spontaneous and some people don't like that. Simple.

The Hank Moody Approach

I wanna be Hank Moody!

Hank Moody is the main character of the show *Californication* of which I am a huge fan and was saddened when it all ended.

I am not trying to be Hank Moody in any way, shape or form but, bearing in mind it is only a television show, tried taking a leaf out of his book of life. His approach is unorthodox to those who are shrinking violets and can only be executed by the very few who are not.

It's all well trying to imitate Hank Moody. The way to be like Hank Moody is to stop trying to imitate Hank Moody because Hank Moody isn't imitating anyone. He has his own unique style and methodology.

I found that apart from the car he drove, I didn't have much in common with him. No, I did not buy my car because Hank drove one, I just happened to work hard and fulfil a schoolboy dream and happened to buy it before I discovered the show.

Hank is the *'I don't care what happens'* free-spirited, occasionally charming, but depending on whom he is with, smoothest person you'll ever see with the ladies. Secretly, I think all guys would like to be like him. I know I would.

Over the years, out of curiosity too I hasten to add, I have read books on being a pickup artist etc. but I noticed very quickly I am not a natural at the 'pickup' game. I can rely on natural charm but will freefall and crash then burn when trying to adopt methodologies as per pickup artists.

Hank Moody, through his charm, demeanour and antics, is able to successfully charm women of all types.

The point trying to be made is that of all of us to some point regardless of sex, would relish being in a position of power and influence in terms of being able to control those who we desire or simply fall head over heels for.

By control, I do not mean dominate, take advantage of, or manipulate, but to be able to take control of the situation by knowing what to say and when to say it and how to say it but not being too generic and thus tailoring it to suit the audience. Audience being the required lady.

I was never a shrinking violet, but would sometimes hesitate unnecessarily and the opportunity that may have presented itself would simply have been and gone and there was nothing I could do about it. Hindsight turned out to be a real best friend!

The approach I adopted did not entail me harassing every single lady in the style of Benny Hill at my chosen venue to a point where the staff and doorman would be informed and subsequent eviction from the premises was guaranteed. However, the approach was emphasising personality traits and to an extent any skillset or hidden talent I may have had. I had to work with what little I had. Be a gambler! Place my bets and hope I struck lucky instead of striking out!

Young at Heart

For me, it was a case of be young at heart but not necessarily immature. This is a Gemini trait and is very much a way I view the world. Being a responsible and mature adult is hard work. There is pressure to conform to the way society as a whole expects you to behave, airs and graces etc., and then there are the ladies of different characters and backgrounds that have to be catered for.

It is just plain old nice to just have some fun and forget responsibilities and loosen up a bit. Actually, loosen up a lot. I therefore approached my quest for women with the mentality that they too need to loosen up. If that is the case, as I have seldom found, then they are most appreciative of a man who can bring her into a child's world where priorities changed albeit for a few hours or a weekend, and generally having some fun and enjoying life was paramount at that moment in time.

I suppose I have found the ladies I have encountered on my journey somewhat relieved and even grateful that they won't be judged on what may come out of their mouths and also by their actions or somewhat spirited behaviour.

Granted this approach has not worked with everyone and rather than be popular like hot cakes, I have been dropped like the hot tray containing the hot cakes that scolded the hands instead.

Carefree and free-spirited

Being carefree and free-spirited can come naturally to some individuals and on the flipside it takes a lot of courage. I have learnt that it is one crucial ingredient in the whole cake mix when it comes to attracting women.

We naturally find it daunting and subsequently become suppressed due to the fact we are so afraid of being judged so quickly and unfairly on what we actually wanted to do or say.

I already knew from an early age that I should not play it cool and wait for a lady, let alone a stunning specimen of the female species, to approach me and initiate some form of eye contact let alone some form of conversation. I am not that calibre of guy.

Contentious point time but – unless you are rich and famous, or exceptionally good-looking, it does not happen. Only in the movies.

My close female friends have mentioned in conversations that they prefer it when the guy will approach. Therefore, I do that very same thing. What is the worst that can happen? She can only say no. It's not as though she will pull out a lethal martial arts combo in the style of video game Mortal Combat and claim flawless victory! Or even worse, have her friends chant "Finish him!"

There are boundaries and space needs to be respected at the same time. However, the approach of carefree and free-spirited is refreshing to some and those ladies will appreciate it.

More Baggage Than Heathrow Terminal 5

Fortunately, I don't consider myself to have any emotional baggage or otherwise. However, close female friends have always advised that when I'm with a lady, I should not bore her with my sensitive problems. I don't. I am surprised at how many are or have been on past dates with other guys.

We are constantly informed in the media or in other formats that ladies, generally speaking, require a strong, mature and sensible, responsible, blah blah man and thus do not want to be bogged down with a man who they pity and has issues. There is being empathetic and that's where it should stop.

From going on numerous dates, the one thing I have been told by ladies when they recall worst dates ever is that any emotional issues should be reserved for the psychiatrist. When a guy is on an initial meet up or a first or even second date with a lady, the advice is not to lay out cards on the table recalling a life story and how you were treated unfairly by parents in comparison to siblings etc.

It is selfish it seems, but the ladies want to forget problems when they're with their gentleman of choice and not be in a position of having to deal with new ones, especially ones that are not their own.

This can work both ways. I naturally would like to be there for that someone special and provide support and almost be that rock that they need, but that could only take place when the relationship has evolved into something special at least, and not after a week.

It Hurts my head when I think!

I have reached that age where my brain went from *"I really shouldn't say that!"* to *"Sod it, let's see what happens if I do!"*

Thinking sometimes hurts, but can also be dangerous and yet exciting at the same time and should only happen once in a while!

I, along with many men, especially in the past, overthink when I'm talking to ladies. Well not anymore! I now tend to say the first thing that pops into my mind. Granted there is a moment of silence post comment being put out there, but subsequently that comment tends to be the funniest they have heard all day. Phew!

Granted I am no comedian, never claimed to be either but the age-old cliché of if you can make a woman laugh springs to mind, then, we are on a good foundation rather than dodgy ground!

I have a sense of humour. I have been told I have a great sense of humour by many, including past dates and girlfriends. It is dry and can be as dry as Gandhi's flip-flops but it is a sense of humour nonetheless. It does not go down well with all but this really all depends on the sense of humour possessed by the desired lady of choice. If she has one, then count myself lucky. However, if not, then good luck or just simply move on. The last thing I wanted was to have my personality stifled and not be allowed to be myself comfortably.

Bad Boy or General Bell End?

On many an occasion I do get asked why I am single. It's a known fact and wonder of the universe that all the nice guys finish last. The Bell End* (bad boy) tends to get the ladies. Fact.

*'Bell End' is an English term used to crudely describe the tip of a man's penis.

I am going to make a very contentious sweeping generalisation that will have some throw up their arms in despair and raise eyebrows. I say this as it has had the very same effect in the past in conversations with friends, associates and work colleagues when this topic is brought up.

There is no such thing as a bad boy. The bad boy is an attribute pertaining to any Hollywood character depending on script. The actors play characters that tend to have something about them that is alluring and possesses an air of mystique that the ladies find intriguing. That is it. That is all it ever will be.

The bad boy wannabes in the real world are just generally talentless Bell Ends. I have noticed on the whole that they have no formal education or qualifications, not that academic excellence is the be all and end all. They tend to have no career prospects, drive or motivation to improve themselves or to do better in life generally. They have no money or assets worth mentioning. They drift along and blame the world and everyone in it for their shortcomings as men. They are not gentleman and most certainly do not know how to conduct themselves like gentlemen. They tend to be abusive to the lady they are with and think nothing of bullying them, whether it be physically or verbally, and treating them like dirt whilst cheating on them with their best friend or sister. Mentally or financially instable or both. A complete gormless erection.

The only time the nice guy gets a look in is when the Bell End has really screwed the lady over and done a disappearing act that would make Lord Lucan or Houdini green with envy.

The nice guy is safe, he is dependable, he is stable financially and mentally, he is out of the friend zone, he is in with a chance! Well... until the next Bell End pops along and then the cycle continues.

Upon having described the above to those who have asked why I am single, to my surprise many a lady has remarked upon how I have accurately described a guy whom their friend, sister or someone close is in fact, much to the annoyance of family and friends, currently dating. Pretty accurate albeit a generalisation.

Initially, Hank Moody may be considered to be a form of bad boy but the difference being he has talent. In the show, he is a gifted and successful writer.

A lot of ladies I have conversed with on the subject have come up with the one common denominator.

They think they can change the bad boy into a gentleman. Films and TV are partially to blame for this.

The guy is a Bell End as described, and then after having met a lady from the other side of town or the tracks as they put it in the movies, the girl somehow falls in love and then tries to convert the guy from a Fiat into a Ferrari of a man. In the movies it works and she gets all the credit and they get married and breed degenerate little shits whom will take after their father and live happily ever after.

In the real world, it only works to an extent up to an Alfa Romeo level. Then the ladies get frustrated due to lack of change as a result of the Bell End being made or asked to change and not wanting to adhere to change. Another vicious cycle.

The other thing Hank Moody and I have in common is that we love women. Naturally, we have fun with them, we engage with them and show genuine sincere interest in them whilst seeking to learn everything about them.

We outrageously flirt with just about any woman like it is second nature, another Gemini trait but on my side more than his, and I believe it is healthy and therapeutic for both parties whether it be as the recipient or flirter.

Dare I say, I have even managed to flirt with more than one lady at the same time like the true Man Whore that I am. Great for building confidence going forwards, but can be a real disaster when it all goes Pete Tong and I risk crashing and burning.

I have learned one thing by observing the group of ladies whilst flirting shamelessly. I really have to find something interesting and funny and quirky even to say. Only then, will I have their attention and open up the possibility to engage furthermore. Whilst engaging I have to ensure I direct my attention evenly and not just at the one I really want. Otherwise, the mobile phones are whipped out. Disaster! The phone extraction becomes a domino effect! One whips out her phone, then the next one, then another one, and thus it continues! They will find it more interesting to respond to a guy they may have been ghosting lately than hear any more! Or even text each other to say *"Let's ditch him and leave this place!"*

Eventually, then the only solitary female left, if not a couple of ladies, is struggling. She really wants to stay and listen. Okay she may not have been my first choice, shallow I know, but her friend or the group are signalling to her. They have known her a lot longer than me and she will have to follow them. Sisters before Misters!

I really did contemplate call this book *The Girl Whisperer!* after one of the characters in *Californication* referred to Hank Moody as being one, after subsequently discovering Hank had not only wooed and slept with his estranged wife, but with many of the other faculty members as well as students whilst amassing a following of female admirers. *Wannabe Girl Whisperer* seemed more appropriate as I was not in that guy's league!

In the style of Hank Moody, I also contemplated calling this book *Life's a Bitch, and Then You Marry One!*, but that would have sounded like I am bitter which I am most definitely not. Hank Moody I think would not have cared and just called it what he wanted without worrying about political correctness.

Sounds dodgy, but only those who have watched the show will resonate.

When it All Goes Pete Tong!

Ladies and Gentlemen! Oh dear oh dear oh dear! I have nothing to add. No wise words or pearls of wisdom to impart upon thee.

For those who deserve it there is:

"It's not me, it's you!"

For those who do not, as ever, the skills of a diplomat are required when not trying to hurt someone's feelings.

As silver-tongued as I like to consider myself to be, I am absolutely shite at this.

How I have pondered and encountered a form of writer's block as someone who is not a writer. Naturally, I have had to tailor the response on the type of person I am dealing with. Dealing with sounds harsh, interacting with sounds more pleasant.

It could be argued that women have it very easy on the dumping. Contentious statement I know but I find it to be true. They can come across as being straightforward without being bitchy and that is that. They can always be a lot bitchier if they want and that is just down to her and how the relationship was.

If the guy adopts the same wording and approach, god help him! He will be cursed, have an effigy or voodoo doll made of him and be labelled a complete arse and have his number displayed in a gay chat line. Thankfully this has not happened to me but it did to a close friend whom I promised to keep anonymous – until he pisses me off! Only kidding.

Thank heavens for the key diplomatic words such as 'Connection', 'Click' and 'Chemistry'. They seem to be more commonplace now when being dumped whether as the dumper or the dumped.

"Although we did initially 'Click', I am really gutted as I really wanted there to be 'Chemistry' and a deeper 'Connection' also. It is something fundamental I am looking for. I hope you understand."

It is such a fantastic way of saying *"You looked much better in the photos and I don't find you attractive in real life!"*

The worst way of being dumped is by text message. I find it to be rude, arrogant and disrespectful. Another snippet of wisdom bestowed upon me by my female friends was never to do that separating by text, despite the fact that I never did or ever would do that anyhow.

I personally always found the parting of ways to be easier either face to face or at worse case over the telephone if distance and time was an issue. As a result, the parting of ways was more amicable and I would always prefer to part on good terms and not be friends with that person rather than part with venom and risk abusive texts or calls post the event.

Contentious statement time again. I have found Indian women tend to be the worst offenders in this case. It's amazing how they seem to be complete naturals at this. If you are very lucky you may get a message similar to the one I use. If not, then you will simply get "It's not working, all the best." That's it. That's all you will get. It is unreasonable to ask for anything more you selfish person.

That and ghosting.

Ghosting is literally the act of suddenly ceasing all communication with someone the subject is dating, but no longer wishes to date. This is done in the hope that the ghostee will just 'get the hint' and leave the subject alone, as opposed to the subject simply telling them he/she is no longer interested. Ghosting is not specific to a certain gender and is closely related to the subject's maturity and communication skills. Many attempt to justify ghosting as a way to cease dating the ghostee without hurting their feelings, but it in fact proves the subject is thinking more of themselves, as ghosting often creates more confusion for the ghostee than if the subject kindly stated how he/she feels.

Quote courtesy of the Urban Dictionary.

Is it really too much to ask of someone to take out five minutes of their time to put someone straight? Not a rant, but a question I have always asked myself and have heard others, female as well as male, who have not fared so well in their quest for love ask the same.

Is the dumper's time and attention too precious, more so than the person who is about to be dumped?

Strange how people on the whole – sweeping generalisation time again– wish for a potential to be intelligent and respectful amongst other qualities and attributes. Yet, the Urban Dictionary highlights key words such as 'maturity' and 'communication skills'.

From conversing with friends, male and female for a more balanced perspective, it seems there a multitude of contributing factors with regards to why it is considered more acceptable to behave in such a way.

The common reasons seem to be:

The person didn't seem interested anymore like they used to, and the task of texting began to feel like a chore and it wasn't worth spending any more time or energy.

One word answers and a raft of emojis (which are not always easy to understand/ interpret) rather than a sentence. From this, it is apparent the other person is having a better conversation with someone else.

The thought of that alone and thinking that the date is having a better time talking to another potential partner is just an enthusiasm quencher. It's as simple as that.

Granted the lack of interesting if not stimulating conversation can drive someone away from continuing communication leading to a potential romance.

I have experienced all the above and will no doubt continue to do so, it's part of the seeking and dating ritual but that was not and still is not an excuse to be rude and Ghost.

A simple "I am really sorry, but I am not feeling any connection and find we don't have anything in common, etc., etc." would be much more appreciated and the other party would get the message a lot sooner rather than guessing. If anything, the sooner the other party is told, the sooner they can move on and find someone more suitable and deserving.

The world of dating in any form would be more fun if it were not for the fear of being rejected and the methodology of the rejection. Not an earth-moving statement I know but it is so simple and so true yet it gets ignored repeatedly. The maturity and communication skills tend to go out of the window.

At the time of writing this, I had stumbled across a couple of articles on MSN that mentioned other types of behaviour known as *'bread crumbing'* and *'zombied'*! I honestly could not believe what I had been reading.

Zombied: It starts off with similar behaviour to ghosting, where someone you have been chatting with goes days without responding or acknowledging your message. In the worst cases, they will visibly 'read' your message and fail to respond. Whatsapp blue tick bitch!

After a while, you might give up on the ghost ('Good riddance', you think) and start talking to someone else. You might even go on dates to move along with your life, until suddenly…

They come back! Yes, risen from the dead, zombie-style.

Bread crumbing: Also known as 'Hansel and Gretelling', offers singletons the glimmer of hope they need to keep the conversation alive. Receiving sporadic but suggestive text messages could be a sign that you're getting bread crumbed. The texter may be attempting to boost their ego by keeping you interested with the minimum amount of effort possible. In serious cases, the person sending the suggestive texts may pop up every few months, only to flit back out of your life after.

Definitions according to MSN.

I had experienced the aforementioned behaviours as a recipient but never knew that there would actually be a term or expression associated with them.

Let's try and bring some dating etiquette, if there is such a thing.

Evolution or Revolution?

Has the world of dating undergone a revolution or simply evolved? It may seem that whatever has happened, has been a tad too quick for our liking, me in particular, and many are struggling to keep up. Will those belonging to the 18–30 be saying the same in 10–15 years? Or will it have slowed down and wait for the next cycle of change. Therefore, dare I say it, I am single in the wrong time era!

There was a time when a couple would simply meet up for a coffee or dinner post meeting up or bumping into each other at a venue or a night out. Whether the pre-date bumping into was facilitated by friend or family doesn't really matter. That post bumping into coffee/dinner would have been called a date.

Based on personal experiences and from conversing with the ladies I have encountered on my love quest, nowadays, it seems to be wrong and presumptuous to call it a date.

The term 'meet up' is a more prevalent term used. The meet up will determine whether, naturally of course, there will be a 'date' that will come out of it.

Again, in the past, post two or three dates, once it could have been said they are 'dating'. How wrong could I be? Very it seems.

Naturally, the process of a relationship evolving (from the male perspective) depends on whom one is interested in. Whether she is an Ice Maiden or a Desperate Doris will determine the stages/phases one will have to pass through and even if one is fortunate enough to skip a level or two due to good behaviour!

Kind of seeing

Once the two or three dates have taken place successfully and all is well with the world, then apparently, you are not dating. No no no! Get those thoughts out of your head dear boy! You are both 'kind of seeing' someone.

This allows freedom for both parties to window shop and grab a last minute deal of a lifetime that would be too good to pass up! Punch above our weight in simple terms.

Just started seeing

This provides a tad more security in a potential relationship. This stage or phase exists when you have made it past the holding hands and fifth date stage or phase.

The term itself inspires and motivates. Although neither party is out of the woods yet, it means you have a chance! Don't blow it!

Dating

Well done fella! You've made it! Well… Almost. She has made a semi-formal commitment. If you are lucky, she may tell the other potential suitors, wannabe bad boy players and lounge lizards she is content.

Content being the key word. There is still ample time and opportunity to cock the whole thing up without realising what's just happened! Then subsequently end up listening to Dido on repeat.

Boyfriend

Congratulations or Commiserations! Depends on whom you have bagged and tagged! A unicorn or a donkey!

Congratulations if one had managed to pass every stage even if not with flying colours but experienced an adventure getting to the end! If one managed to skip a few levels from a simple meet up and obtained a fast track promotion to boyfriend level, then kudos to you.

Commiserations if one had an arduous and sometimes perilous journey and just about scraped through every stage whilst contemplating giving up and pursuing a new challenge. Even worse is when the sudden realisation dawns upon them that you are now at a level of commitment albeit not as concrete as fiancé or husband.

Just like a game show host would exclaim *"Look at what you could have had!"* the term will ring in ones ears as they spot a deal or bargain that they overlooked or had missed out on or should've waited for.

Most will interpret the above as a bit of a cynical perspective I can imagine, but I have unfortunately found this to be more and more accurate nowadays.

Everyone seems to be holding out for something better it seems. A bit like a car owner regardless of whether their pride and joy be a classic, sporty number or quirky and of an acquired taste.

Unless they are smitten with their dream ride and will never get rid no matter what happens, most are of the mindset *'Yep, keep this one for a bit, see what's out there and if it gives me any trouble, then I shall get rid quick time! There are bound to be better ones out there.'*

Apparently, if you want to believe everything that is read on the internet, nearly half of women have a backup partner. This can be a guy who is a 'close friend', great on paper but didn't quite get the job as he was either underqualified or had applied too late.

Regardless, the application was kept on file and will be retrieved from the filing system as and when a suitable vacancy arises.

Lessons Learnt

Such a popular phrase nowadays. Synonymous with politicians and those in positions of authority for when it all goes Pete Tong!

What have I learnt? Anything at all?

To be honest, apart from the obvious stuff I knew beforehand, not much. Ok, I jest. I have learnt a little bit. The little I have learnt is scary but has not put me off dating ever again. Well… not yet anyhow.

It has been a great learning curve and experience. If I had a time machine and went back to a younger version of me, say 26 years old, and explained what the score was, I think I would have just laughed at my older self and ridiculed accordingly. In fact, I probably would not have believed it could be so tricky and now be considered an art to be able to initially attract a lady, make her swoon, have her wanting to come back for more and then obtain her complete devotion and have her forsake all others. Well for the time being at least.

From the perspective of the guy, regardless of creed, colour ethnicity on both parts, I think it is much harder and the ladies have it a tad easier. Only a tad. Yet another contentious sweeping generalisation but my last one though.

Unless the guy is for arguments sake, Brad Pitt, George Clooney or David Beckham (many other Hollywood heartthrobs, rock and sports stars are available), most of us mere mortal men have to jump through many hoops and pull out rabbits from hats amongst other magic tricks to exceed sometimes unrealistic benchmarks set by ladies.

The ladies have the upper hand it seems and those ladies whom I have asked this very question seem to answer with *'not really'* but with a wry smile simultaneously.

That means *'Of course we do! We are just not going to admit it!'*

Like it or lump it, the game of dating has changed and the rules of dating that go with it.

We can either adapt to the new way or hope that we find someone in more a traditional way with whom we can communicate face to face rather than behind a screen or via phone messaging.

Now for the *Jerry Springer* style final thought. This came to me whilst sat in a meeting at work talking about budgets for a new car and my mind started to wonder. Without meaning to brag, I am both shocked and impressed I managed to come up with this. Flipping awesome!

The flame on the dating candle will flicker and sometimes wane or shrink. I've learnt not to let it die out. It's had its moments. Keep it going despite the urge to blow it out completely wanting to take over. Have faith and let the intense energy of the flame burn bright for all to see. Hopefully someone will see it, love it and want it.

Lightning Source UK Ltd.
Milton Keynes UK
UKOW01f2019190218
318150UK00001B/340/P